5—

W9-DCJ-231

Holiday
Scrapbooking

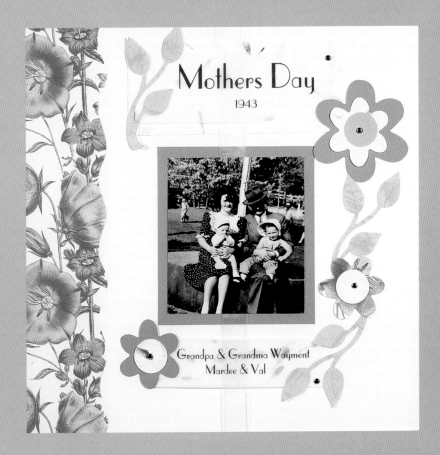

200 Page Designs

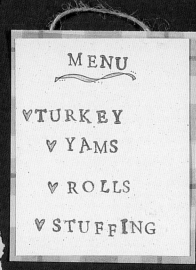

MENU

♥TURKEY

♥ YAMS

♥ ROLLS

♥ STUFFING

GIVE
THANKS

NOV 2000

Holiday Scrapbooking

200 Page Designs

Vanessa Ann

Sterling Publishing Co., Inc.
New York
A Sterling / Chapelle Book

Chapelle, Ltd:
Jo Packham, Sara Toliver, Cindy Stoeckl
Cathy Sexton, Editor
Karla Haberstich, Art Director
Kim Taylor, Graphic Illustrator
Marilyn Goff, Copy Editor

Staff:
Kelly Ashkettle, Areta Bingham, Ray Cornia,
Emily K. Frandsen, Susan Jorgensen, Barbara
Milburn, Lecia Monsen, Karmen Quinney,
Desirée Wybrow

Photography:
Kevin Dilley for Hazen Imaging, Inc.

Library of Congress Cataloging-in-Publication Data
Ann, Vanessa.
Holiday scrapbooking : 200 page designs / Vanessa Ann.
     p. cm.
ISBN 1-4027-0677-4
1. Photograph albums. 2. Photographs--Conservation and
restoration. 3. Scrapbooks. 4. Holiday decorations. I. Title.
TR465 .A56 2003
745.593--dc21
                                              2003010219

10 9 8 7 6 5 4 3 2 1

Published by Sterling Publishing Co., Inc.
387 Park Avenue South, New York, NY 10016
© 2003 by Vanessa Ann
Distributed in Canada by Sterling Publishing
c/o Canadian Manda Group, One Atlantic Avenue, Suite 105
Toronto, Ontario, Canada M6K 3E7
Distributed in Great Britain by Chrysalis Books
64 Brewery Road, London N7 9NT, England
Distributed in Australia by Capricorn Link (Australia) Pty. Ltd.
P.O. Box 704, Windsor, NSW 2756, Australia
Printed in China
All Rights Reserved

Sterling ISBN 1-4027-0677-4

If you have any questions or comments or would like
information on specialty products featured in this
book, please contact:
Chapelle, Ltd., Inc.
P.O. Box 9252
Ogden, UT 84409
(801) 621-2777 • (801) 621-2788 Fax
e-mail: chapelle@chapelleltd.com
web site: www.chapelleltd.com

The written instructions, projects, and photographs
in this volume are intended for the personal use of the
reader. Any other use, especially commercial use, is
forbidden under law without the written permission
of the copyright holder.

Every effort has been made to ensure that all the
information in this book is accurate. However, due
to differing conditions, tools, and individual skills,
the publisher cannot be responsible for any injuries,
losses, and/or other damages which may result
from the use of the information in this book.

CONTENTS

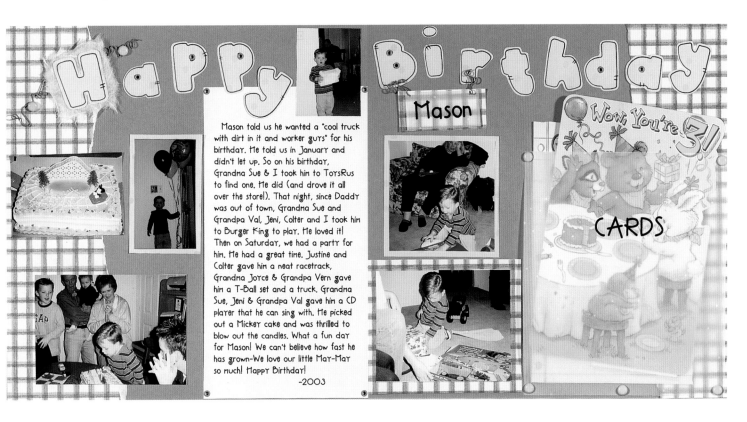

Happy Birthday

Mason

Wow, You're 3!

CARDS

Mason told us he wanted a "cool truck with dirt in it and worker guys" for his birthday. He told us in January and didn't let up. So on his birthday, Grandma Sue & I took him to ToysRus to find one. He did (and drove it all over the store!). That night, since Daddy was out of town, Grandma Sue and Grandpa Val, Jeni, Colter and I took him to Burger King to play. He loved it! Then on Saturday, we had a party for him. He had a great time. Justine and Colter gave him a neat racetrack, Grandma Joyce & Grandpa Vern gave him a T-Ball set and a truck. Grandma Sue, Jeni & Grandpa Val gave him a CD player that he can sing with. He picked out a Mickey cake and was thrilled to blow out the candles. What a fun day for Mason! We can't believe how fast he has grown-We love our little May-May so much! Happy Birthday!

-2003

Welcome to another volume of scrapbooking page designs.

This book was written on the premise that you already know the basics of scrapbooking—from knowing how to use the basic tools to being familiar with simple techniques such as photo matting.

As you have probably already figured out, scrapbooking is a very personal form of art and can be presented on many different levels. Some scrapbookers want their scrapbooks to be absolutely precise with all of their pictures perfectly aligned on the page, photo mats cut with exact precision, and journaling to be done to perfection. Other scrapbookers enjoy a more relaxed look and feel to their pages—using torn-paper photo mats and page borders, natural fibers such as raffia and jute, and all of the cutting and placement done simply without a lot of fuss.

The page designs presented here are from the scrapbooks of a few distinguish scrapbookers! We hope this volume will encourage, motivate, and teach as you embark on some new designs and ideas. So, sit back, relax, and start cropping!

—Vanessa Ann Designers

The pages presented in this volume were created in a double-page format on both 8¹/₂" x 11" and 12" x 12" pages. Each spread includes a complete supply list for creating the featured pages and is accompanied by a design tip or idea.

Because the pages presented here have been created with many fun dimensional objects, such as beads, buttons, brads, and ribbons, the archival-quality of the scrapbook pages has been compromised. You will also want to use page protectors that have been specifically designed for this type of scrapbooking and store these albums upright. We very much encourage you to keep your treasured archival volumes separate from your fun, day-to-day dimensional albums.

Easter egg Hunt

The weather was perfect for this years easter egg hunt. The kids had a great time. We were able to use the upper park at Mt. Ogden, so we could hide the eggs in the trees! I don't think we ever found all of the eggs, but it was fun for the adults to finish the search! After we were finished, we had a great lunch from KFC. When we got home, Justine & Colter decided to make bunny ears and paint their faces. They were so cute—we had to take a picture! Happy Easter!
—1997

Choosing an Adhesive

There are several archival-quality adhesives on the market that work great for scrapbooks. The trick is finding the one best suited to you and your style of scrapbooking.

When adhering photographs to cardstock for matting purposes, double-sided adhesive tabs are widely used. Glue sticks also work well and are inexpensive. They are however messier to use.

When attaching dimensional objects, such as buttons, scrapbook glue is recommended. This type of adhesive is a heavy-duty glue manufactured specifically for this purpose.

Journaling

Journaling on your pages is probably the most important element when scrapbooking.

Some scrapbookers are hesitant to do much journaling because they either don't like their handwriting or they aren't quite confident enough to know what to write or how to write it. Don't let these fears deter you—there is nothing more special than personalizing something in one's own handwriting and dialect. This gives added enjoyment when the scrapbooks are passed from generation to generation.

Handwritten vs Computer-generated Journaling

There are pros and cons to both methods of journaling, but handwritten journaling adds the finishing touches to the personalization of the project. Many scrapbookers would prefer to use a computer for their journaling because they don't believe their handwriting is nice enough. Other scrapbookers wouldn't dream of using anything but their own penmanship on their pages—another confirmation that scrapbooking is a unique art form based strictly on the individual taste of the scrapbook artist.

Some of the pages in this volume have been hand-lettered. On the pages that have been computer-generated, the sentiments were typed and then printed directly on a full sheet of vellum or cardstock. It is impossible to put scraps of cardstock through your printer. In addition, keep in mind that many printers cannot accommodate the thickness of a sheet of cardstock, so hand-lettering may be your only option. One alternative is to print your sentiments out on bond paper—white or colored—then adhere it to cardstock.

An important point to consider when choosing between handwriting and computer-generated journaling is which of the methods is archival. Unless you have the luxury of printing from a laser printer, the best choice would be handwriting. Ink-jet printers are not archival quality and over time the ink will fade and can actually chip off the page. Handwriting done with archival journaling markers is timeless.

Ring out the old, ring in the *new,*

Ring *happy* bells, across the snow:

The *year* is going, let him *go;*

Ring out the *false,* ring in the *true.*

—Alfred Tennyson

Designed by Kim Garner

SUPPLIES
Background Paper:
    Sage Green with Swirls
Layout Cardstock:
    White, Recycled White
Vellum: Clear
Fibers: White
Pewter Year Block
Adhesive
Journaling: Computer

Use famous quotes to highlight the theme of your scrapbook pages. When using computer-generated journaling, use a variety of fonts to help emphasize important words or phrases.

"Ring Out the Old"

Carefully tear the cardstock around the words so each word is on a separate piece. Randomly adhere each word on top of the fibers.

Designed by Kim Garner

SUPPLIES
Background Cardstock: Navy Blue
Layout Cardstock: Silver, White
Patterned Paper: Navy Blue with Stars
Die-cut Letters
Star Charms: Silver
Eyelets: Steel Blue
Craft Wire: Navy Blue
Tinsel: Metallic Silver
Adhesive
Journaling: Navy Blue Marker

"Midnight Magic"

Attach decorative accessories, such as tinsel, to your scrapbook pages with an acid-free glue that dries transparent.

"Happy New Year"

Designed by Paige Hill

SUPPLIES
Background Cardstock: Black
Layout Cardstock:
    Black, Metallic Gold, White
Patterned Papers:
    Brown/Tan Stripes,
    Brown Renaissance Print
Die-cut Letters & Numbers
Brads: Gold-toned
Star-shaped Brads: Gold-toned
Embroidery Floss: Metallic Gold
Micro Hole Punch
Craft Wire: Black
Tinsel: Metallic Gold
Adhesive
Journaling: Computer

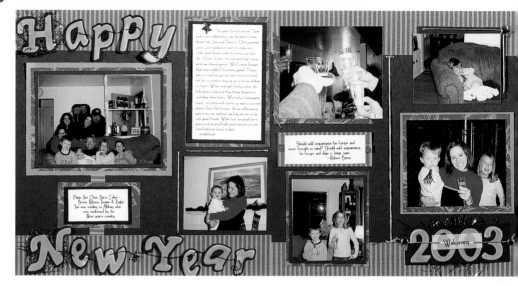

"Metallic" is a terrific highlighting factor for scrapbook pages. Use metallic paper for die-cut letters, metallic tinsel to accent certain areas, and metallic thread to define certain spaces.

"Chinese New Year"

Designed by Karen Delquadro

SUPPLIES
Background Cardstock: Black
Layout Cardstock: Black,
    Red, White
Stickers: Chinese New Year
    Assortment, Fireworks,
    Numbers
Miniature Chinese New Year
    Paper Lamp
Rubberstamp: Chinese Symbol
Ink Pad: Black
Embroidery Floss: Metallic Silver
Fibers: Black, White
Adhesive
Journaling: Black Marker

When creating special themes for your scrapbook pages, use decorative items to emphasize what that theme is. For example, use Chinese symbols and stickers in an Oriental theme.

"Just Add Snow"

Designed by Kim Garner

SUPPLIES

Background Cardstock: Navy Blue
Layout Cardstock: White
Patterned Paper: Powder Blue
   with Snowflakes
Handmade Papers: Orange, White
Vellum: Clear
Fibers: Black, White
Pewter Snowman Charm

Hat, Mittens & Trees
Craft Foam: Black
Buttons: Medium Blue
Twigs
Craft Wire: Navy Blue
Adhesive
Journaling: Black Marker

When assembling accessories to be used on your scrapbook pages, use your creativity and a variety of craft mediums such as handmade paper, craft foam, craft wire, and buttons.

"Building a Snowman"

Designed by Karen Delquadro

SUPPLIES

Background Cardstock: Kraft
Layout Cardstock:
    Black, Brown, Dark Red, White
Patterned Paper: Black with
    Heads of Snowmen,
    Red/Black Plaid
Fibers: White
Precut Tags: White

Pewter Snowman Charms
Alphabet Beads: White
Heart Bead: White
Mini Brads: Black
Button: Green
Chalk: Black
Adhesive
Journaling: Computer, Black Marker

Torn-paper artwork is a creative addition to any scrapbook page. When tearing cardstock into various-shaped pieces and assembling them to create images such as a snowman or a Dalmatian dog, use chalk on the torn edges for shading and definition.

Designed by Karen Delquadro

SUPPLIES
Background Cardstock: Dark Red
Layout Cardstock: Kraft,
    Dark Red, White
Laser-cut Stickers
Rubberstamps: Lower Case Alphabet
Ink Pad: Black
Pewter Letter "V" Block
Paper Punch
Die-cut Primitive Heart
Mini Brad: Black
Primitive-heart-shaped Brads:
    Pink
Glass Hearts
Eyelets: Red
Metal Frame: Gold-toned
Ribbon: Ivory
Embroidery Floss: White
Adhesive
Journaling: Black Marker, Pink Marker

"Making Valentine Cards"

Using your scrapbook supplies for other purposes is certainly allowed. Here, a gathering to make valentine cards to exchange ends up being a wonderful event to scrapbook the memories.

Designed by Paige Hill

SUPPLIES
Background Cardstock: Kraft
Layout Cardstock: Red
Patterned Paper: Valentine Sentiments
Handmade Papers:
    Red, Off-white with Embedded Flowers
Vellum: Clear
Chalk: Red
Die-cut Primitive Hearts
Mesh: Red
Mini Brads: Gold-toned
Heart-shaped Brads: Gold-toned
Craft Wire: Gold-toned
Open Heart Confetti: Red
Adhesive
Journaling: Computer

"Sweet Hearts"

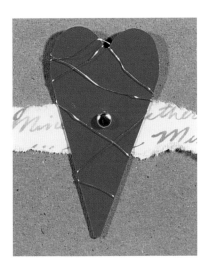

Craft wire can be used as a decorative element on any scrapbook page. Use it to wrap around various-shaped die-cuts, then attach them to your scrapbook page with mini brads.

Happy Valentines
Day

bruce was out of town again this year
for Valentines Day, so it was just the
boys & I. We decided to go to the mall
with mom, dad & mardee. We ate
dinner and did some shopping. When we
got home, there was a bouquet of flowers
from bruce sitting on the porch! They
were absolutely beautiful! The next night
for bruce's arrival home, Cotter made a
cute little display for him on our
kitchen table. He is such a sweetheart!
How lucky I am to have such great
men in my life. And bruce, no matter
how far he travels, he always is
thinking of me, and me of him. Happy
Valentines!

-2002

my Love

"Happy Valentine's Day"

Designed by Paige Hill

SUPPLIES

Background Cardstock:
   Recycled Sandstone
Layout Cardstock: Cayenne
Handmade Paper: Dark Brown
Vellum: Clear
Heart Charms with Words: Red
Craft Wire: Silver-toned

Mini Brads: Silver-toned
Straw Flower Heart
Potpourri Sachet Bag
Sewing Thread: Red
Sewing Machine
Adhesive
Journaling: Computer

Use your sewing machine to apply embellishments to your scrapbook pages. A variety of stitches can be used, but it is always best to use cardstock as your background because of its strength.

"Bee My Valentine"

Designed by Karen Delquadro

SUPPLIES
Background Cardstock:
   Recycled White
Layout Cardstock: Black, Dark Red
Blank Puzzle
Stickers: Eye, Letters
Punches:
   Heart, Puzzle Piece, $3/4$" Square
Bumblebee
Adhesive
Journaling: Black Marker

When using puzzle pieces on your scrapbook pages, embellish each piece to captivate your audience's attention. Add "stitch" lines around the outer perimeter of each puzzle piece with a marker to add clarity and definition.

"My Funny Valentine"

Designed by Karen Delquadro

SUPPLIES
Background Cardstock: Recycled Red
Layout Cardstock: Baby Pink,
   Light Pink, Dark Red, Recycled Red
Stickers: Laser-cut Hearts, Letters
Mesh: Red
Mini Brads: Black, Red
Heart-shaped Button: Gold-toned
Paper Punch
Punch: Primitive Heart
Square Metal-rimmed Tag
Circle Swirl Paperclip
Ribbon Scraps
Straight Pin
Thread: Metallic Gold
Adhesive
Journaling: Black Marker

To accent the outer perimeter of any torn object or matted photograph, outline with a marker using a decorative method such as a combination of lines, dashes, and dots.

Designed by Paige Hill

SUPPLIES
Background Cardstock: Recycled White
Layout Cardstock: Red
Patterned Papers: Brown with Leaves,
    Ivory with Embossed Swirls
Vellum: Clear
Die-cut Primitive Hearts
Mini Brads: Gold-toned
Craft Wire: Red
Sheer Ribbon: Red
Adhesive
Journaling: Computer

"Be My Valentine"

Place your scrapbook page title and your journaling information on strips of vellum. Attach the vellum strips to your scrapbook pages with mini brads positioned at each corner or with an adhesive that is appropriate for use on vellum. Try using colored cardstock or graphics behind your vellum strips.

"Valentine Kisses"

Designed by Kim Garner

SUPPLIES
Background Cardstock: Black
Layout Cardstock: Black, White
Vellum: Mauve, Metallic Pink, Metallic Silver
Craft Wire: Pink, Silver-toned
Adhesive
Journaling: Silver Marker

Christian loves his little sister, Sydnee, so much. He is so kind and gentle with her... most of the time. I always knew they would love each other, I never thought I would witness that love. These pictures give a glimpse.... Dec. 2002

Bend craft wire into the shapes of letters to accessorize your scrapbook pages. A child's name or a special sentiment can be used. Additional wire shapes, such as hearts, can be added.

Designed by Karen Delquadro

SUPPLIES
Background Cardstock: Red
Layout Cardstock: Off-white
Vellum: Clear
Square Metal-rimmed Tags: Clear Vellum
Mini Brads: Gold-toned
Stickers: Letters & Numbers
Heart-shaped Buttons: Gold-toned
Mesh: White
Adhesive
Journaling: Black Marker

"My Valentine"

Cut vellum into the desired dimensions. Adhere the piece of vellum to your background cardstock as desired. Layer the mesh on top of the vellum and secure in place with an appropriate scrapbook adhesive.

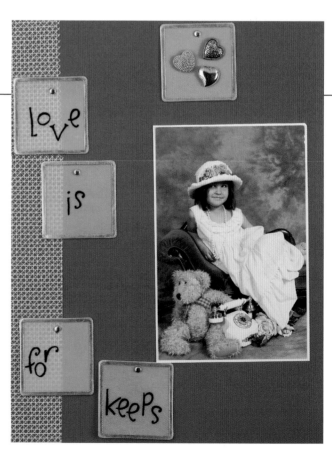

"Valentine's Dance"

Designed by Cindy Stoeckl

SUPPLIES
Background Cardstock: Red
Layout Cardstock: Pink
Patterned Paper:
    White with Tiny Red Hearts
Preprinted Artwork: Flying Cupid Pig
Die-cut Curved Hearts
Foam Adhesive Dots
Adhesive
Journaling: Metallic Gold Marker,
    White Pencil

Accent die-cuts that have been punched from plain cardstock by drawing designs on them with metallic-colored markers. Dots, vertical and horizontal lines, and squiggly designs work well. Adhere to your scrapbook pages with foam adhesive dots so the hearts "beat" off the page.

"Easter Delight"

Designed by Kim Garner

SUPPLIES
Background Paper: Pastel Plaid
Layout Cardstock: Yellow Plaid
Alphabet Template
Mini Brads: Gold-toned
Embroidery Floss: White
Miniature Clothespins
Adhesive
Journaling: Blue Marker, Pink Marker

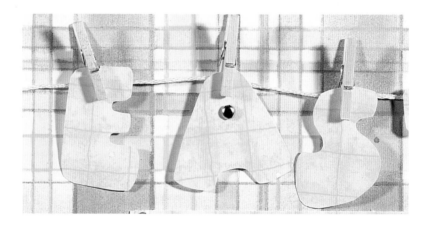

Trace letters from an alphabet template, then cut them out. Place one miniature clothespin at the top of each letter, thread embroidery floss through the clothespins, and hang the word or phrase in a clothesline fashion across the top of your scrapbook pages.

Designed by Karen Delquadro

SUPPLIES
Background Cardstock: Pastel Pink
Layout Cardstock: Pastel Blue,
    Gold, Pastel Green, Olive Green,
    Orange, White, Pastel Yellow,
    Yellow
Punches: Egg, Letters & Numbers
Fibers: Multicolored
Adhesive
Journaling: Black Marker

Cut a small triangular-shaped piece from orange cardstock to make a beak for each letter and number. Adhere one beak to each letter and number. Add an eye to make each letter and number look like a baby chick.

Designed by Kim Garner

SUPPLIES
Background Cardstock:
    Sky Blue
Layout Cardstock: White
Patterned Papers: Soft Green
    with Muted Dots,
    Yellow Checks
Vellum: Green
Alphabet Template
Punch: Flower
Buttons: Assorted Colors
Embroidery Floss: Beige
Adhesive
Journaling: Black Marker

When using letters cut from an alphabet template, position a few of the letters "backward." Then, instead of cutting a hole in the letters that have openings, use a small button in its place.

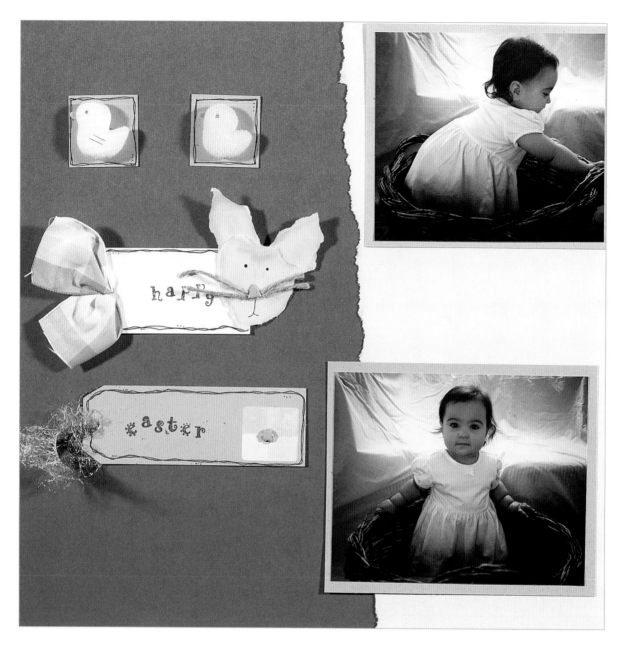

"Happy Easter"

Designed by Karen Delquadro

SUPPLIES

Background Cardstock: Navy Blue
Layout Cardstock: Pastel Blue, Ivory,
    Kraft, Pastel Pink, Putty, White
Rubberstamps: Lower Case Alphabet
Ink Pad: Black
Fibers: Multicolored
Natural wool
Jute: Natural
Stuffed Ducklings

Triangular-shaped Brad: Pink
Flower-shaped Brad: Pink
Punches: Bunny, Large Square
Eyelets: Pink
Ribbon: Pink Plaid
Assorted Buttons: Ivory, Pink
Adhesive
Journaling: Black Marker

Use alphabet rubberstamps and a black ink pad to title your pages and/or do the journaling. Do not worry if you are unable to perfectly align the letters.

Use a variety of mediums, such as jute, fibers, and ribbons, to attach "tags" to your scrapbook pages.

Easter

This Easter we went to brunch at Webby's grill. We were so lucky to have Matt, Aleisha, Grace and Ivy with us. After we ate, we went to Mardee's to play in the park and enjoy visiting with our family. The weather was beautiful. The kids had so much fun sliding, swinging and playing basketball. When it was time to go, Mason had to give Ivy a love! It was so cute!
-2002

Designed by Paige Hill

SUPPLIES
Background Cardstock: Pastel Pink
Layout Cardstock: Lavender, Mint, Pink
Patterned Paper: Pastel-colored Stripes
Vellum: Clear
Punch: Flower
Brads: Peach
Mini Brads: Silver-toned
Paper Punch
Sheer Ribbon: Lavender
Adhesive
Journaling: Computer

"Easter at the Park"

The shape of a simple punch, such as a flower, can add so much to the overall look of any scrapbook page. Place one flower at opposite corners of your photographs, or combine two or three in various colors to form a floral cluster.

Easter's here!
The bunny's hopping,
heralding the joys
of spring.

-Jan Miller Girando

Designed by Paige Hill

SUPPLIES
Background Cardstock: Lavender
Layout Cardstock: Steel Blue, Mint Green,
    Olive Green, Lavender, Peach, Pink,
    White, Yellow
Vellum: Clear
Punches: Egg, Flower, Primitive Heart,
    Primitive Star
Brads: Assorted Colors
Mini Brads: Gold-toned, Silver-toned
Flower-shaped Eyelets: Purple
Burlap: Natural
Jute: Natural
Sheer Ribbon: Mint Green
Ribbon: Yellow
Embroidery Floss: Orange
Craft Wire: Yellow
Adhesive
Journaling: Computer, Black Marker

"Easter Fun"

Punch out several various colored eggs. Embellish each one to transform it into a wonderful decorated Easter egg. Heart and star punch-outs, adhered with a mini brad, make a great embellishment. Flower-shaped eyelets are especially decorative and come in a wide assortment of colors.

Grandpa England & the Grandkids.

Easter
For this year's Easter celebration, there was a party at the Plain City Park for the entire England family. This was a bittersweet time, as my Grandfather was activated shortly after the holiday. The kids posed for pictures before heading out for fun.
--1945

"Easter 1945"

Designed by Paige Hill

SUPPLIES

Background Cardstock: Periwinkle
Patterned Paper: White with
    Large Butterflies
Vellum: Clear, Clear with Butterflies
Brads: Lavender

Sheer Ribbon: Lavender
Eyelets: Lime Green
Craft Wire: Silver-toned
Adhesive
Journaling: Computer

Cut butterflies from the patterned paper and the patterned vellum. Place the butterflies randomly on your scrapbook pages and bend craft wire into antennae.

Designed by Karen Delquadro

SUPPLIES
Background Cardstock: Vanilla
Layout Cardstock: Bright Pink,
    Pastel Pink, White
Patterned Cardstock:
    Red & Off-white Plaid
Precut Tag: White
Silk Ribbon: Soft Rose
Jewels: Pink
Chalk: Pink
Adhesive
Journaling: Colored Markers

"Bunny Ears"

Use colored chalk to define an area or subject. Use it sparingly or generously depending on the amount of highlighting and/or shading you are trying to achieve.

Designed by Cindy Stoeckl

SUPPLIES
Background Cardstock:
    Vintage Wallpaper Pattern
Layout Cardstock: Mauve, Pink
Vellum: Green
Preprinted Artwork: Easter Egg, Tag
Stickers: Vintage Easter Assortment
Sheer Ribbon: Lavender
Adhesive
Journaling: Green Pencil

"Easter Games"

Cardstock is available in various patterns that look like vintage wallpaper. If you cannot find cardstock such as this, simply color-copy a piece of your favorite wallpaper, then adhere the color copy to a piece of cardstock for added stability.

Designed by Kim Garner

SUPPLIES
Background Cardstock: White
Layout Cardstock: Purple
Patterned Papers: White with Lavender
   Stripes, Sage Green with Muted Dots
Assorted Buttons: Shades of Lavender
Adhesive
Journaling: Purple Marker

"You Are My I Love You"

I am your way home;
   You are my new path.
I am your dry towel;
   You are my wet bath.
I am your calm face;
   You are my giggle.
I am your wait;
   You are my wiggle.
I am your dinner;
   You are my chocolate cake.
I am your bedtime;
   You are my wide awake.
I am your favorite book;
   You are my new lines.
I am your nightlight;
   You are my star shine.
I am your lullaby;
   You are my peekaboo.
I am your goodnight kiss;
   You are my I love you.
      — Maryann K. Cusimano

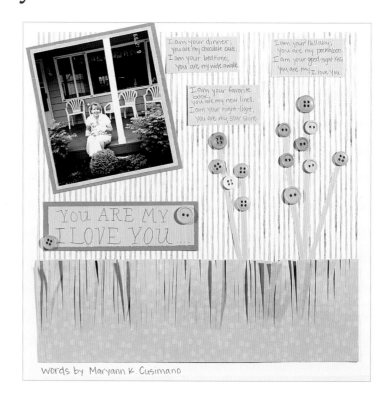

Designed by Kim Garner

SUPPLIES
Background Cardstock: Sage Green
Layout Cardstock: Dark Green
Patterned Paper: White with Sage Leaves
Punch: Large Leaf
Adhesive
Journaling: Gold Marker

"A Mother's Love"

Punch a row of leaves from the sheets of dark green cardstock. Position one of the punched sheets on the background cardstock vertically and position the remaining punched sheet horizontally. Adhere the leaf punch-outs randomly on the photo mats.

"Mother's Day"

Designed by Paige Hill

SUPPLIES

Background Cardstock: Moss Green
Layout Cardstock: Olive Green,
  Pastel Lavender, Mint, Pastel Pink,
  Light Plum, White
Vellum: Clear
Mini Brads: Silver-toned
Punch: 1" Square

Flower Charms
Eyelets: Moss Green
Die-cut Primitive Hearts
Micro Hole Punch
Craft Wire: Silver-toned
Adhesive
Journaling: Computer

This mothers day, Colter gave me the cutest framed print, he had printed his favorite things about me. Number one was that I do his laundry! Pretty funny. We then went to brunch at Roosters . We had a great meal & loved visiting with our family. We always reflect on all of the good times we have had. The surprise gift came from Jeni. She claims to not have a creative bone in her body, yet she made the most beautiful card -complete with hand made paper! It was a beautiful day, almost as beautiful as my mom. She is more than just a parent; she is one of my best friends. Everything I know about being a good mom to my kids, I learned from her. Thanks mom!

May 12th, 2002

" A mother's love for her child is like nothing else in the world. It knows no law, no pity, it dares all things and crushes down remorselessly all that stands in its path."

-Agatha Christie

Geometric shapes add tremendous impact when used in repetition. Use several squares punched from cardstock to border your scrapbook pages. If desired, add additional embellishment, such as die-cuts or charms, on top of one or more of the squares.

Mothers Day

We had a wonderful brunch at Roosters for Mothers Day. Aleisha, Matt & Grace came up from California. It was great to be able to finally see Grace in person! She is such a sweet baby. The kids and Bruce got me a beautiful gift basket-Bruce even gave me a card from Groucho! It was a beautiful day, so after brunch we all went to our house to play outside. Happy Mothers Day!

-1997

Designed by Paige Hill

SUPPLIES
Background Cardstock:
    Floral Wallpaper Pattern
Layout Cardstock: Pink, Pastel Pink,
    Pastel Yellow
Patterned Cardstock:
    Floral Wallpaper Pattern
Vellum: Clear
Mini Brads: Silver-toned
Alphabet Beads: Silver-toned
Sheer Ribbon: Light Pink
Foam Adhesive Dots
Adhesive
Journaling: Computer

"Mother's Day Brunch"

This is one of my favorite pictures. I love how beautiful Mom is and how sweet Justine and Grace are.

Use foam adhesive dots to elevate decorative elements on your scrapbook pages that you want to call special attention to. In addition to creating a three-dimensional look, it allows you to overlap motifs.

Designed by Karen Delquadro

SUPPLIES
Background Cardstock: Gold
Layout Cardstock: Medium Blue, Navy Blue,
    Pastel Blue, Dark Brown, Recycled
    Buckskin, Green, Olive Green, Ivory,
    Soft Moss, Periwinkle, Pink, Red,
    Tan, White
Patterned Paper: White with Floral Fibers
Punches: Cloud, Small Flower,
    Primitive Heart, Snowflake
Mini Brads: Black
Heart-shaped Brad: Red
Micro Hole Punch
Embroidery Floss: Black
Adhesive
Journaling: Computer

"I Love Being Your Mom"

Hanging signs are fun to use and can be a great way to use up cardstock scraps. Cut your scraps into several squares with the exact dimensions. Embellish each square as desired. Punch tiny holes at each corner of the tops and bottoms of each square; the square that will be at the bottom of the hanging sign should have holes punched at the top corners only. Thread embroidery floss through the holes, knot at the top, and attach to the scrapbook page with a mini brad.

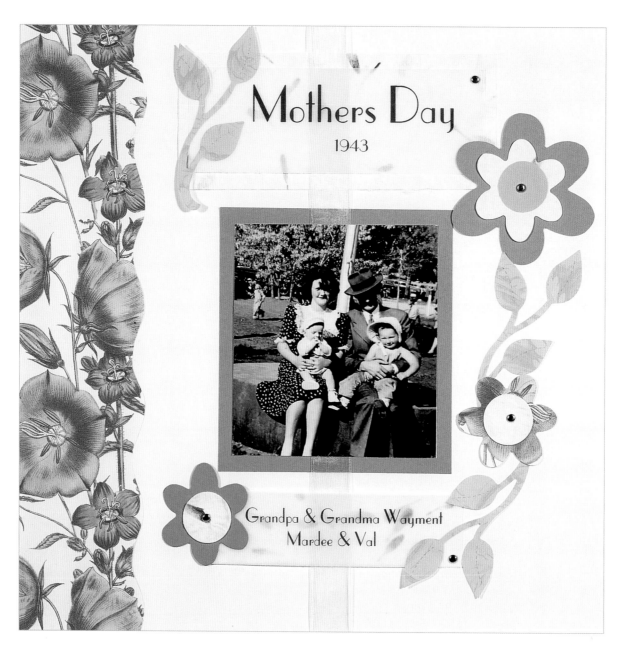

"Mother's Day 1943"

Designed by Paige Hill

SUPPLIES

Background Cardstock: Ivory
Layout Cardstock: Dusty Lavender
Patterned Paper: Ivory with
   Large Lavender Flowers,
   Ivory with Small Lavender
   Flowers, Olive Green with Swirls
Handmade Paper: White with
   Embedded Flowers

Vellum: Clear
Mini Brads: Silver-toned
Sheer Ribbon: Lavender
Punch: Large Circle
Die-cut Flowers: Medium, Large
Die-cut Leaves on Vine
Adhesive
Journaling: Computer

Grandma England &
The Grandchildren.

Grandpa England &
The Grandchildren.

On Mothers day, The England
family had a picnic at the Plain
City park. All of the children were
able to come and visit. It was a
beautiful day, sunny and warm.

-1943

Color is such an important element on any scrapbook page. Use colors that will set the mood for the
theme of your pages. In this case, the feminine colors
in delicate hues were chosen.

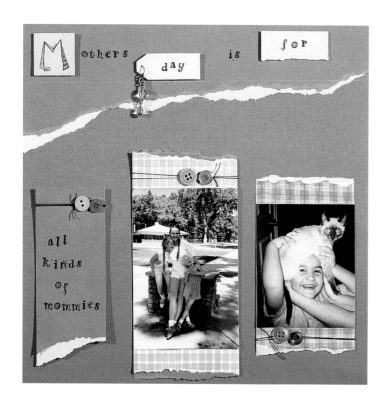

Designed by Karen Delquadro

SUPPLIES
Background Cardstock: Brown
Layout Cardstock: Navy Blue, Olive Green,
  Pastel Green, Sage Green, Pastel Pink,
  Putty, Red
Patterned Paper: White with Blue Plaid and
  Small Flowers, Green Plaid, Red Plaid,
  Pink Heart Gingham
Rubberstamps: Lower Case Alphabet
Ink Pad: Black
Embroidery Floss: Black
Assorted Buttons: Assorted Colors
Beaded Dangle
Adhesive
Journaling: Black Marker

"All Kinds of Mommies"

Tear several colors of cardstock and layer as desired. Make certain each layer is hand-torn so it creates a significant decorative element.

"My Hero"

Designed by Karen Delquadro

SUPPLIES
Background Cardstock: Recycled Tan
Layout Cardstock: Dark Brown, Tan
Patterned Paper: Brown Brocade
Preprinted Artwork
Ribbon: Beige with Leaves & Berries
Sheer Ribbon: Brown
Assorted Buttons: Brown
Pewter Photo Frames
Adhesive
Journaling: Black Marker

Use preprinted artwork of "scrabble" game pieces, or the actual game pieces, for a unique way to journal your scrapbook pages with adjectives describing any special person or memorable event.

To Mother

Cards

Mothers Day

Grandpa surprised Grandma with portraits of the kids for Mothers Day. He got them all dressed up and took them down town. On Mothers Day the kids got up early and made her breakfast. When breakfast was over, they presented her with homemade cards and the portraits. She was truly surprised. Grandma treasured these photographs throughout her life. The next day, Grandpa sent her some flowers just to remind her how special she is everyday—not just on Mothers Day. How true that is.

—1951

"Children are the anchors that hold a mother to life."

Sophocles

"Mother's Day 1951"

Designed by Paige Hill

SUPPLIES

Background Paper: Beige with Powder Blue Flowers and Scrolls
Layout Cardstock: Metallic Blue
Vellum: Clear, Clear with Flowers, Blue & White Gingham

Mini Brads: Silver-toned
Sheer Ribbon: Mint Green
Decorative Flowers on Wires
Adhesive
Journaling: Computer

Memorabilia, such as the card that accompanies a delivered bouquet of flowers, is wonderful as scrapbook page adornment. You will find that many of these vintage items have discolored with age; this will add to your overall expression.

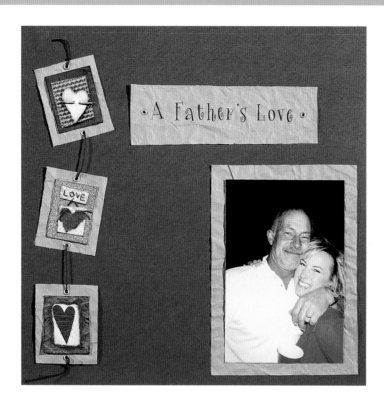

Designed by Kim Garner

SUPPLIES
Background Cardstock: Burgundy
Layout Cardstock: Moss Green
Preprinted Artwork: Quilted Hearts
Stickers: Letters
Eyelets: Copper
Embroidery Floss: Burgundy
Adhesive
Journaling: Black Marker

Mat a piece of preprinted artwork with cardstock, then position one eyelet at the top and one eyelet at the bottom. Repeat with a few more pieces of printed artwork. String each piece together with multiple strands of embroidery floss.

"A Father's Love"

Designed by Karen Delquadro

SUPPLIES
Background Cardstock: Brown
Layout Cardstock: Brown, Ivory, Kraft,
    Sage Green
Patterned Paper: Green Gingham
Rubberstamps: Lower Case Alphabet
Ink Pad: Brown
Fibers: Multicolored
Jute: Natural
Embroidery Floss: Olive Green
Stickers: Heart, Stars
Chalk: Brown, Green
Adhesive
Journaling: Brown Marker

"I Love My Dad"

Cut tags in various sizes from different colors of
cardstock. Stamp a word or phrase on each tag.
Highlight and accent the tags with chalk.

Fathers day
We planned a fishing trip to the Uintah Mountains for Fathers Day weekend. The Grandpas had a great time fishing at Lily Lake. Rather than fish, Aleisha and I spent our time decorating the pine trees to look like Christmas trees. It was great to have both sets of Grandpas together for Fathers Day. We had a great time.
—1974

Grandma Hansen & the old van

"Father's Day Fishing Trip"

Designed by Paige Hill

SUPPLIES

Background Cardstock: Dark Brown
Layout Cardstock: Olive Green, Recycled White
Patterned Paper: Buckskin Suede, Brown Stripes
Vellum: Clear

Eyelets: Large Gold-toned
Jute: 3-ply Natural
Mini Brads: Gold-toned
Preprinted Artwork: Fish
Adhesive
Journaling: Computer

Grandpa Wayment

Dad

"I cannot think of any need in childhood as strong as the need for a father's protection." — Sigmund Freud

Grandpa Hansen

Vertically tear the center section from a sheet of background cardstock. Place a sheet of patterned paper in the center of the piece of cardstock. Position one eyelet at the inner corners of the cardstock pieces. Thread jute through the eyelets and tie into a knot.

"Dad"

Designed by Karen Delquadro

SUPPLIES

Background Cardstock: Kraft
Layout Cardstock: Dark Brown,
  Brown, Kraft, Pumpkin
Patterned Paper: Tan with Spatters
Rubberstamps: Lower Case Alphabet
Ink Pad: Brown
Jute: Natural

Assorted Buttons:
  Brown, Ivory
Miniature Wrench
Meshes: Brown
Adhesive
Journaling: Computer

There is only one kind of love,
but a thousand different versions...

La Rochefoucauld
French moralist 1613 – 1680

I have always looked at my dad in awe,
he was strong and stoic, he seemed
bigger than life to me as a child.
   As I grew into an adult, I began
to see him in a different way, his
expectations of me never seemed
out of reach, there was great
pleasure in seeing his pride in my
achievements, he said to me
once... "I'm proud of you kid"..
it still means the world to me,
his open affection was rarely given
and I knew he meant it.
   He loved my child, I saw him
in a way I never had before, He was
tender/affectionate, he needed her love
and she brought out the best in him.
   I miss his quirky sense of humor,
his integrity, and the sound of his laughter
in the room still fills my heart with joy!

Mesh comes in several different sizes and colors. Use
a variety of different sizes on the same scrapbook
page by placing it over sections of cardstock.

There are only TWO reasons why YOU are the GREATEST DAD...

one

two

"You Are The Greatest Dad"

Designed by Kim Garner

SUPPLIES

Background Cardstock: Olive Green
Layout Cardstock: Recycled Tan,
Recycled White, White
Fibers: White
Assorted Buttons: Assorted Colors
Craft Wire: Silver-toned

Mini Brads: Silver-toned
Glass Beads: Clear
Pewter Year Block
Adhesive
Journaling: Computer

Adhere glass beads over words you have chosen to magnify. Words can be written on plain colored papers or on lightly patterned papers. Small images, such as a butterfly, can also be cut out and used in place of words.

"Happy Birthday"

Designed by Kim Garner

SUPPLIES
Background Cardstock: Yellow
Layout Cardstock: Blue, Lime Green, Yellow
Cardstock Scraps: Assorted Colors
Die-cuts: Balloons, Party Hats, Happy Birthday
Craft Wire: Copper-toned
Beads: Multicolored
Adhesive
Journaling: Black Marker

Die-cuts are dynamic when layered. Accent your die-cuts by adding shadows, such as on balloons or by embellishing, such as adding colorful dots to a party hat. Some scrapbook supply outlets have die-cuts available for purchase that are already layered.

"Birthday Bash"

Designed by Kim Garner

SUPPLIES
Background Cardstock:
    White
Layout Cardstock:
    Blue, Green, Red
Patterned Papers: Red with
    Multicolored Dots, White
    with Multicolored Stripes
Die-cut Letters
Circle Metal-rimmed Tags
Adhesive
Journaling: Assorted Markers

When working with color combinations, such as primary colors, mat each photograph in a separate color of cardstock to coordinate with the colors in your scrapbook spread.

"Birthday Balloons"

Designed by Karen Delquadro

SUPPLIES
Background Cardstock:
    Purple
Layout Cardstock:
    Pastel Blue, Pink,
    Red, Yellow
Die-cut Balloons:
    Assorted Colors
Preprinted Artwork: Birthday
Fibers: White
Adhesive
Journaling: Computer

Adhere the balloon strings only where they meet the knotted ends of the balloons. This allows the strings to hang freely and look more realistic.

"Happy Birthday Gracie"

Designed by Paige Hill

SUPPLIES

Background Cardstock: Pink with Embossed Flowers, Soft Moss with Embossed Swirls

Layout Cardstock: Same as Background Cardstock

Patterned Paper: Variegated Pink Gingham

Handmade Paper: Pink
Vellum: Clear
Stickers: Floral Alphabet
Brads: Pink
Eyelets: Yellow
Adhesive
Journaling: Computer

See the single candle,
on the birthday cake?
I am turning one year old,
and this is no mistake.

Use a sheet of patterned cardstock as the background on one side of your scrapbook spread. Use a contrasting pattern as the layout cardstock. Reverse the concept for the remaining side of your scrapbook spread.

"Make A Wish"

Designed by Kim Garner

SUPPLIES
Background Cardstock:
 White
Vellum: Blue, Green, Pink,
 Purple, Yellow
Punch: Swirl
Adhesive
Journaling: Black Marker

Use colored vellum to mat your photographs. Try using a separate color for each one. Use scraps of the colored vellum to cut strips in various heights and widths to make the candles. Add the flame at the top of each candle with a swirl or spiral punch.

"Lexee's 2nd Birthday"

Designed by Kim Garner

SUPPLIES
Background Cardstock:
 White
Layout Cardstock:
 Pastel Green, Pastel
 Lavender, Pastel Pink,
 Pastel Yellow
Preprinted Artwork:
 Birthday Assortment
Eyelets: Assorted Colors
Adhesive
Journaling: Purple Marker

Cut a four-petal flower from the pastel pink cardstock to make the frosting on each cupcake. Cut a rectangular-shaped piece of cardstock from the pastel yellow cardstock, then accordion-fold it to look like a cupcake paper liner. Make the candle from pastel green cardstock with a pastel yellow card-stock flame. Add the "sprinkles" on the cupcake with colored eyelets randomly positioned.

"Mason's Big Day"

Designed by Paige Hill

SUPPLIES
Background Cardstock:
  Blue
Layout Cardstock:
  Red, Yellow
Vellum: Clear
Brads: Blue, Red
Micro Hole Punch
Craft Wire: Blue
Adhesive
Journaling: Computer,
  Black Marker

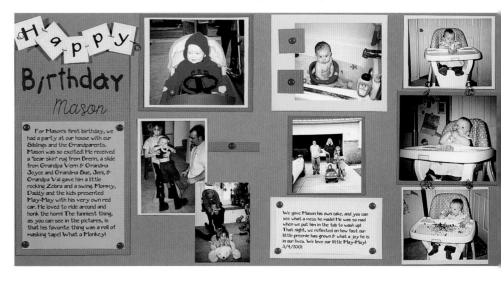

There is nothing more lifting than bright colors. Use primary colors on your scrapbook pages featuring children for a perfect combination.

"I'm Finally Six"

Designed by Paige Hill

SUPPLIES
Background Cardstock:
  Blue
Layout Cardstock:
  Orange, Red
Preprinted Artwork: Birthday
Eyelets: Blue, Lime Green
Brads: Blue
Adhesive
Journaling: Computer

Preprinted artwork doesn't always have to be purchased. Try cutting motifs out of old greeting cards.

My 1st Birthday

My first birthday was a big event.
Our little house was full of people!
Some memorable gifts I received
were "Flatsey" Dolls, a talking
phone, clothes and a Mother Goose
doll. My mom baked a cute circus
cake and a small cake for me to dig
into. I had to include this picture of
me in the tub, getting washed up
after my cake mess. I'm sure it was
a great party!

-August 2, 1971

"My 1st Birthday"

Designed by Paige Hill

SUPPLIES

Background Paper:
   Baby Pink/Light Pink Stripes
Layout Cardstock:
   Mint Green, Pastel Pink, White
Patterned Paper: Mink Green with
   Embossed Pink Roses

Mini Brads: Silver-toned
Alphabet Beads: Silver-toned
Sheer Ribbon: Mint Green
Adhesive
Journaling: Computer

Thread alphabet beads that spell out a name or special sentiment onto lengths of sheer ribbon. Attach to your scrapbook pages by placing a mini brad at each end of the word or sentiment to secure the beads close together.

Grandma England's
81ˢᵗ Birthday

We had a big party for Grandma
England when she turned 81. I was only
five months old at the time. Grandma
England was my Grandma Wayment's
mother. She was a neat lady. She lived on
her own until she was 86 years old. Her
house was built in the 1900's and had an
outhouse. Whenever we would go visit,
we would catch water skeeters in the
ditch in front of her house. She made
everything from scratch (including
mayonnaise) and was an expert quilter.
The stitches in the quilt she made me
when I was born are perfect-amazing
since she was 80 when she quilted it! She
passed away in 1990 at the age of 99. She
outlived four of her seven children and
was a widower for almost 40 years. What
an amazing woman.

January 14, 1972

Beautiful

"Beautiful Grandmother"

Designed by Paige Hill

SUPPLIES

Background Paper: Ivory with
    Pink French Print
Layout Cardstock:
    Baby Pink, Light Pink
Patterned Paper:
    Same as Background Paper
Vellum: Clear

Sheer Ribbon: Pink
Paper Roses
Eyelets: Large Gold-toned
Mini Brads: Gold-toned
Craft Wire: Gold-toned
Adhesive
Journaling: Computer

Ribbon can be added to your scrapbook pages. Try knotting the center of a length of sheer ribbon, then fold each end back and forth two or three times. Secure the ribbon ends in place with mini brads. Another alternative is to knot the center of a length of sheer ribbon, leaving a loop at the top of the knot. Place the ribbon streamers to each side making a "swag-like" embellishment across the top of your photograph.

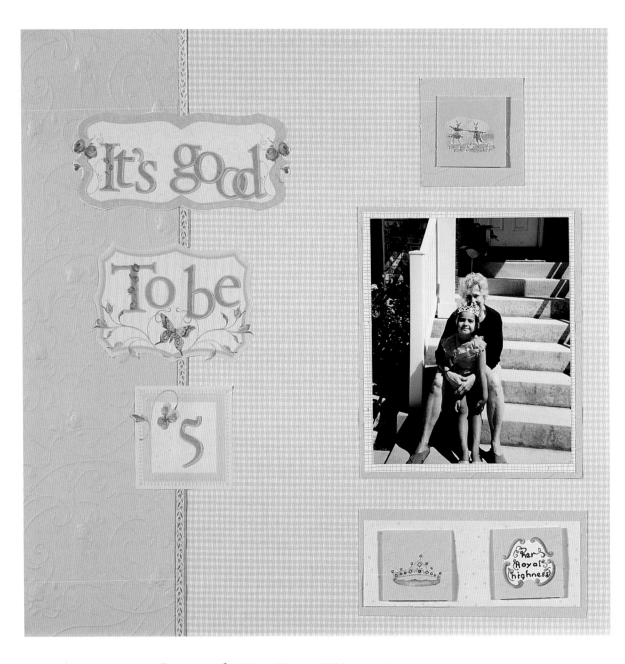

"It's Good To Be Five"

Designed by Karen Delquadro

SUPPLIES

Background Cardstock:
  Pink Gingham
Layout Cardstock: Soft Moss
  with Embossed Swirls
Patterned Paper:
  Off-white with Squiggly
  Pink Lines, Pink with Tiny Dots
Stickers: Floral Alphabet,
  Floral Frames,
  Salutation Assortment
Preprinted Artwork:
  Birthday Assortment
Adhesive
Journaling: Computer

Using decorative-edged scissors, cut photo corners from the layout cardstock. If you prefer straight edges, punch squares from the cardstock, then cut them in half diagonally so each one is the exact size.

Designed by Karen Delquadro

SUPPLIES
Background Cardstock: Navy Blue
Layout Cardstock: Gold, Pink,
    Pastel Pink, White
Stickers: Letters, Vertical Stripes
Preprinted Artwork: Birthday Assortment
Fibers: Multicolored
Punch: Circle
Micro Hole Punch
Adhesive
Journaling: Black Marker

"Hanna's 5th Birthday"

When making "letter" blocks to spell out a word, such as "BOWL-ING," use an art image in the place of one or more of the letters. A bowling ball is the perfect substitute for the letter "O."

Designed by Paige Hill

SUPPLIES
Background Cardstock: Blue
Layout Cardstock: Kraft
Vellum: Clear
Preprinted Artwork: Hawaiian Assortment
Brads: Blue, Pink
Micro Hole Punch
Jute: Natural
Adhesive
Journaling: Computer

"Happy Hula Birthday"

Using preprinted artwork is a great way to provide the theme for your scrapbook pages. Embellishing pre-printed artwork will further enhance your pages. Punch tiny holes into the center of each flower on the preprinted lei, then thread jute through each hole. Knot at the top and tie the ends into a bow.

"Tea Party"

Designed by Paige Hill

SUPPLIES

Background Paper: Ivory
Layout Cardstock:
    Blue, Navy Blue, Periwinkle
Patterned Paper:
    Blue & Tan Stripes, Ivory
    with Small Blue Flowers
Preprinted Artwork:
    Birthday Assortment,
    Flower Assortment, Tea Cup

Stickers: Letters
Circle Metal-rimmed Tags
Rubberstamps: Lower Case Alphabet
Ink Pad: Black
Fibers: Blue, Green
Embroidery Floss: Black
Adhesive
Journaling: Black Marker

When working with stripes, placed in a vertical position, cut along one of the stripes, separate, then adhere so the background cardstock shows through. Do this randomly so each side of your scrapbook spread is different.

For her girls July birthday's, Cathy had a huge carnival! It was so much fun. She had the older kids in the neighborhood help out. Justine was a fortuneteller & Sarah worked the beanbag toss. The kids had to spend their tickets to play the games and go on the "rides" (the trampoline and airplane stroller—pushed by Lee). Colter spent most of his tickets at the fishpond, but he and Justine did go for a spin on the "airplane". After the carnival, the girls opened presents and all the kids enjoyed cupcakes and snow cones. Happy Birthday!

—July 1999

"Birthday Carnival"

Designed by Paige Hill

SUPPLIES

Background Cardstock: Purple
Layout Cardstock:
    Gold, White
Patterned Cardstock:
    Red with Embossed Dots
Vellum: Clear

Circle Metal-rimmed Tag
Eyelets: Purple
Craft Wire: Gold-toned
Metallic Confetti
Adhesive
Journaling: Computer

Happy hearts and happy faces,
Happy play in grassy places,
That was how, in ancient ages,
Children grew to kings and sages.

Many times the photographs you are using on your scrapbook pages are very "busy." This requires a simple scrapbook page design in order that the viewer won't have trouble distinguishing what is depicted in each photograph.

Happy Birthday
Colter!

For Colter's first birthday party, we
invited friends and family to Jaycee
Park for pizza, cake and ice cream.
Colter had a great time. He loved all of
his new toys & playing with the kids
at the park. We had a great time.

August 24, 1994

"Happy Birthday Colter"

Designed by Paige Hill

SUPPLIES

Background Cardstock:
   Dark Red
Layout Cardstock: Ivory
Patterned Papers: Blue, Red
   & Yellow Plaid, Tan Stripes,
   Vintage Toy Collection

Mini Brads: Gold-toned
Adhesive
Journaling: Computer

Cut several motifs from a vintage toy collection patterned paper to use as scrapbook page embellishments. Randomly position them as desired. This is a great way to use a favorite piece of patterned paper that is too busy to use as a background. This can also be done with other themed papers such as holidays and weddings and those with baby motifs.

"Feliz Cumpleanos"

Designed by Paige Hill

SUPPLIES

Background Paper: Navy Blue
Layout Cardstock: Cayenne,
    Maize, Olive Green, Tan
Paper Punch
Punches: Extra Large Swirl,
    Large Swirl
Alphabet Template

Eyelets: Large Red
Brads: Green, Yellow
Mini Brads: Gold-toned
Micro Hole Punch
Craft Wire: Metallic Green
Adhesive
Journaling: Computer

Alphabet templates are available in many different lettering styles. When you find one that will compliment your scrapbook pages, cut the letters from cardstock. Mat each letter individually with a contrasting color of cardstock. A second mat with yet another contrasting color of cardstock can also be used.

"Spooky Stuff"

Designed by Paige Hill

SUPPLIES
Background Cardstock: Brown
Layout Cardstock: Cinnamon, Pumpkin
Patterned Paper: Orange Plaid
Handmade Paper: Brown
Preprinted Artwork: Pumpkins
Mini Brads: Gold-toned
Craft Wire: Green
Adhesive
Journaling: Computer

Highlight one of the preprinted pumpkins by backing it with a scrap of brown handmade paper, then placing it on a square of pumpkin cardstock. Place one mini brad in each corner. Coil a length of green craft wire around a pencil, then stretch it out to make a "pumpkin vine." Adhere the vine to the top of the pumpkin.

"Haunted Halloween"

Designed by Kim Garner

SUPPLIES
Background Cardstock:
    Orange
Layout Cardstock: Orange
Rubberstamps:
    Upper Case Alphabet
Ink Pad: Black
Assorted Die-cuts:
    Bat, "Boo," Frightened Cat,
    Ghost, Haunted House,
    Tree, Witch on Broom
Fibers: Black
Adhesive
Journaling: Black Marker

Die-cuts are available in just about any image you can imagine. Combine several die-cuts that depict the same holiday on your scrapbook spread. This is a simple, yet effective way to embellish any scrapbook page.

"Clowning Around"

Designed by Karen Delquadro

SUPPLIES
Background Cardstock:
    Mustard
Layout Cardstock:
    Black, White
Stickers:
    Halloween Assortment
Fibers: Black
Candy Corn Buttons
Tiny Buttons: Orange
Star Brad: Gold-toned
Adhesive
Journaling: Black Marker

Make borders on your scrapbook pages with unusual objects. Remove the shanks from the backs of the candy corn buttons. Randomly adhere the buttons down one side of each of your scrapbook pages. Then, affix black fibers down the pages, weaving it in and out and between the candy corn.

"Trick-or-Treat"

Designed by Paige Hill

SUPPLIES

Background Cardstock: Black
Layout Cardstock: Black, Kraft,
    Pumpkin, White, Yellow
Patterned Paper:
    Orange Plaid, Purple Plaid
Vellum: Clear
Alphabet Template
Craft Wire: Purple

Eyelets: Silver-toned
Embroidery Floss: Black, Green,
    Orange, Purple, Yellow
Embroidery Needle
Jute: Natural, Orange
Assorted Buttons: Lavender, Orange
Adhesive
Journaling: Computer, Black Marker

Use an embroidery needle threaded with embroidery floss to "sew" words or phrases onto your scrapbook pages. It is always best to sew onto cardstock because of its strength.

"Spook Party"

Designed by Karen Delquadro

SUPPLIES
Background Cardstock: Purple
Layout Cardstock: Black,
    Kraft, Purple, White
Patterned Vellums: Moon &
    Stars, Spider Webs
Stickers: Halloween Assortment,
    Letters & Numbers
Die-cut Witch's Cauldron
Square Metal-rimmed Tag:
    Clear Vellum
Paper Punch
Micro Hole Punch
Eyelets: Black
String: White
Chalk: Gray
Ultrafine Glitter: Mint
Adhesive
Journaling: Black Marker

Lightly apply scrapbook glue to the areas you want to accent with glitter. Generously sprinkle ultrafine glitter onto the glue and let the glue dry. Remove the excess glitter.

"Ghosts, Witches & Creepy Spiders"

Designed by Karen Delquadro

SUPPLIES
Background Cardstock:
    Black, Hunter's Orange
Layout Cardstock: Black,
    Soft Moss Green,
    Hunter's Orange
Mesh: Black, Orange
Strings: Black, Off-white
3D Spiders
Die-cut Spider Web
Micro Hole Punch
Colored Pencils
Adhesive
Journaling: Black Marker

Use string as an art medium. Use white string as cat whiskers and black string as witch's hair.

"Boo To You"

Designed by Karen Delquadro

SUPPLIES
Background Cardstock:
    Black
Layout Cardstock: Green,
    Orange, Tan, Yellow
Stickers: Bat, Cat, Fall Leaves,
    Letters, Snake, Spider
Tiny Buttons: Orange
Tinsel: Metallic Black
Craft Wire: Brown
Adhesive
Journaling: Black Marker

Torn-paper art can be very challenging, yet very rewarding. Tear orange cardstock into various shaped pieces to create the shape of a pumpkin. Tear the stem from tan cardstock and the leaf from green cardstock. Wrap a length of brown craft wire around a toothpick, then remove, to make the pumpkin vine.

"Happy Haunting"

Designed by Kim Garner

SUPPLIES
Background Paper:
    Black with White Lines
Layout Cardstock:
    Lime Green, Orange
Alphabet Template
Craft Foam: Black
Die-cut Spider Webs
Fibers: White
Embroidery Floss: White
Plastic Spiders: Lime Green
Adhesive
Journaling: Black Marker

Craft foam gives a fun dimension to your scrapbook pages and is very easy to use. Simply trace the letters or desired shapes onto the foam and cut out with scissors. Craft foam is available in different size sheets and comes in a variety of colors.

Halloween

This Halloween, My mom made me this great "Wonder Woman" costume. No small task considering I was in Hawaii with Dad and Grandma Wayment at the time! We got back just in time to Trick-or-Treat. She also made Tobin and Jeni's Dracula capes. I love the picture of the pumpkin at the dinner table. It reminds me of the homemade chili that Grandma made for us each Halloween. We would eat a huge bowl before going Trick-or-treating. It was great!

-1970

"Halloween 1979"

Designed by Paige Hill

SUPPLIES

Background Cardstock:
   Recycled Tan
Layout Cardstock: Black
Patterned Paper:
   Burnt Orange with
   Black Spatters

Vellum: Orange
Eyelets: Large Butterscotch
Brads: Black
Craft Wire: Copper-toned
Adhesive
Journaling: Computer

Dracula #1
(Tobin)

Dracula #2
(Jeni)

Genie
(Aleisha)

Wonder Woman
(Paige)

Compiling mini scrapbooks of special dates and events can make memorable gifts. For example, make a mini scrapbook with the photos of all the Halloween costumes your daughter wore as she was growing up. Present this to her on your granddaughter's first birthday.

HalloWeen

For Hanna's First HalloWeen, We dressed her up Like a pumpkin. She Looked so cute! Jacob Wanted to be Buzz (of course)! He Loved his costume so much; he Wore it For three days straight! On the day before HalloWeen, We carved pumpkins, and then John and I Went to pick out our costumes For the Taylor's annual party. I thought We Made the perfect angel and Devil. HalloWeen night, We trick-or-treated, then Went to the party. WHen We got there, Jacob Was surprised to see that Adam had dressed up as Woody! What a pair they Made! Happy HalloWeen!

--2002

"Happy Halloween"

Designed by Paige Hill

SUPPLIES

Background Cardstock: Black
Patterned Paper:
    Orange Fabric with Brown
    Patches, Tan Stripes
Vellum: Clear
Preprinted Artwork:
    Halloween Assortment

Sheer Ribbon: Orange with
    Black Edges
Brads: Orange
Craft Wire: Dark Green
Adhesive
Journaling: Computer, Black Marker

There are several papers on the market that resemble fabrics, from simple denims to elegant brocades. Some even have patches or special quilting stitches as part of the overall design.

"Our 1st Thanksgiving"

Designed by Kim Garner

SUPPLIES
Background Paper: Gold with
    Red Tri-dots
Layout Cardstock: White
Patterned Paper:
    Red/Gold Large Plaid
Preprinted Artwork: Photo Frame,
    Thanksgiving Assortment
Die-cut Oak Leaves
Colored Pencils
Adhesive
Journaling: Computer

When using fonts that have "open" letters, color the open areas with colored pencils.

"Helping Grandma Stuff the Bird"

Designed by Karen Delquadro

SUPPLIES
Background Cardstock:
   Pumpkin
Layout Cardstock:
   Dark Brown,
   Harvest Gold,
   Olive Green
Stickers: Numbers
Punch: $1/2$" Square,
   1" Square
Mini Brads: Black
Adhesive
Journaling: Computer

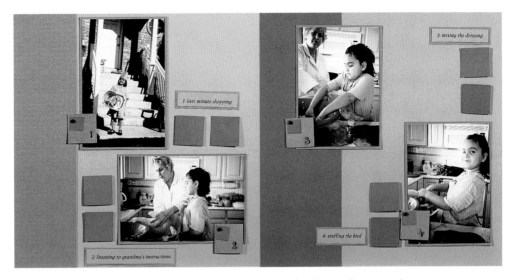

Photo numbering can be done on scrapbook pages that have photographs that need to be placed in order of sequence. Add a number sticker next to each one for an easy visual depicting the order of the event.

"Count Your Many Blessings"

Designed by Kim Garner

SUPPLIES
Background Cardstock:
   Kraft
Layout Cardstock: Rust
Patterned Paper:
   Rust Stripes
Stickers: Acorns,
   Leaf Assortment,
   Thanksgiving Sentiments
Adhesive
Journaling: Computer

Don't always place your matted photographs straight on your scrapbook pages. Try angling and overlapping for added interest.

"Fall Blessings"

Designed by Kim Garner

SUPPLIES
Background Cardstock:
   Harvest Gold
Layout Cardstock: Olive Green
Patterned Paper: Fall Leaves
Precut Tag: Manila
Leaf Buttons: Assorted Colors

Craft Wire: Copper-toned
Mini Brads: Silver-toned
Adhesive
Journaling: Computer

Buttons can be found in a variety of shapes. Leaf buttons are the perfect embellishment for your scrapbook pages with an autumn theme. Attach buttons to your scrapbook pages with craft wire threaded in and out of the button holes, then secured with mini brads at each end.

Thanksgiving 1996
This year, we had dinner at Grandma Joyce and Grandpa Vern's. We were honored to have Grandma Hill & Grandma Benton as our guests. Joyce cooked a wonderful meal that everyone loved. After dinner, we picked up Justine and went to visit Grandma Sue & Grandpa Val. Justine was more than happy to pose for a picture, since she wasn't able to be in our family picture earlier. We had a great dessert of Pie and enjoyed the company of our family.

"Thanksgiving Pilgrims"

Designed by Paige Hill

SUPPLIES

Background Cardstock: Dark Brown
Layout Cardstock: Dark Brown,
    Olive Green, Rust, White
Cardstock Scraps: Assorted Colors
Alphabet Template
Burlap: Natural

Brads: Gold-toned
Craft Wire: Copper-toned
Embroidery Floss: Dark Brown
Adhesive
Journaling: Computer,
    Black Marker

Use burlap to make a great backdrop for your scrapbook pages. Cut it into the appropriate-sized piece and adhere it with a transparent scrapbook glue. Cardstock strips and/or letters can be glued on top of the burlap as desired.

"Turkey Day"

Designed by Karen Delquadro

SUPPLIES

Background Cardstock: Kraft
Layout Cardstock: Dark Brown,
   Harvest Gold, Kraft
Rubberstamps: Lower Case Alphabet
Ink Pad: Black
Stickers: Leaf Assortment

Miniature Clothespins
Eyelets: Brown
Jute: Natural
Mini Brads: Black
Adhesive
Journaling: Black Marker

Labeling can be a great way to journal your scrapbook pages. Stamp several key words or phrases onto scraps of cardstock, cut them out, and mat them. Adhere each label to your scrapbook pages with an appropriate adhesive. Attach the finishing touches with miniature clothespins.

For their Thanksgiving party at Pre-school, Lindsey & Colter got to dress up like Indians and sing the song "The Pilgrims & the Indians". Colter loved his Indian get up and the song. On Thanksgiving Day, Colter wore his Indian headband, leather vest & even brought his bow & arrow (which he kept in his shark backpack)! He entertained everyone with his song, complete with hand motions. It was so cute!

–1998

"Lil' Indians"

Designed by Paige Hill

SUPPLIES

Background Paper: Dark Brown with Leaves & Berries
Layout Cardstock: Brown, Rust, Recycled White
Patterned Paper: Tan with Wheat Stalks

Paper Punch
Eyelets: Large Gold-toned
Jute: Natural
Mini Brads: Gold-toned
Adhesive
Journaling: Computer

The Pilgrims & the Indians
The Pilgrims & the Indians had a
Pow-wow a long time ago. The Pilgrims
& the Indians felt like having a party
& so. The Pilgrims & the Indians cooked a
turkey & Indian corn. Sat down & ate
together and that is how Thanksgiving
was born.

—Janeen Brady

Page headers can be an important element on any scrapbook page. Tear a piece of paper, layered with a torn piece of cardstock, then layered with a rectangular-shaped cut piece of cardstock. Add a vertical strip of cardstock between the second and third layer and attach it to the background paper with mini brads. Punch one hole at each side of the rectangular-shaped piece of cardstock and add one large eyelet at each side of the background paper. Thread a length of jute through each eyelet and each punched hole. Knot as desired.

"Thanksgiving 1951"

Designed by Paige Hill

SUPPLIES

Background Paper: Olive Green Mottled

Layout Cardstock: Dark Brown, Olive Green Embossed

Patterned Paper: Ivory with Acorns & Leaves

Vellum: Clear

Paper Punch

Ribbon: Taupe

Adhesive

Journaling: Computer

Whenever vintage photographs are included, make certain the names and relationship of each person is listed. Sometimes this is done on the back of the photograph. If such information is not included, it takes only one generation for no one to know "who these people are."

Designed by Kim Garner

SUPPLIES
Background Cardstock:
   Tan
Layout Cardstock: Dark Brown,
   Burgundy, Forest Green
Stickers: Letters
Brads: Gold-toned
Adhesive
Journaling: Black Marker

"Season's Greetings"

Display your holiday greeting cards in a mailbox. Cut the stand from dark brown cardstock, the mailbox from forest green cardstock, and the flag from burgundy cardstock. Attach the flag with brads, then layer and adhere your cards as desired.

TO GRANDMOTHER'S HOUSE WE GO

Grandma has always had a special place in her heart for her grandkids. No matter what, everyone always tries to get back to Grandma's house at Christmas time....

Designed by Karen Delquadro

SUPPLIES

Background Cardstock:
    Recycled Red
Layout Cardstock: Ivory, Green,
    Red, Dark Red, White
Cardstock Scraps: Assorted Colors
Stickers: Christmas Balls, Letters
Circle Punch
Metal-rimmed Tags
Eyelets: Green
Craft Wire: Silver-toned
Embroidery Floss: Black
Adhesive
Journaling: Computer, Black Marker

"To Grandmother's House We Go"

Use metal-rimmed tags in an unusual way. Embellish each tag with a separate letter, then add a single eyelet centered at the top of each tag. Spell out the desired phrase and use craft wire to thread the tags together. Don't worry if your tags are not all the same size.

Designed by Karen Delquadro

SUPPLIES
Background Cardstock:
    Olive Green
Layout Cardstock: Black, Red
Stickers: Letters
Punch: Primitive Heart
Mini Brads: Black, Green
Eyelets: Green
Embroidery Floss: Black
Adhesive
Journaling: Black Marker

"Santa Baby"

Use the same motif in repetition on your scrapbook pages. Make certain to use them randomly for added impact.

Designed by Kim Garner

SUPPLIES
Background Cardstock: White
Layout Cardstock: Burgundy, White
Patterned Paper: Red/White Plaid
Die-cut Letters
Stickers: Merry Christmas
Eyelets: Red
Pewter Sleigh Charm
Primitive Heart: Silver-toned
Raffia: Red
Chalk: Red
Adhesive
Journaling: Black Marker

"Believe"

Chalk can be a wonderful medium to use for scrapbooking. Use it to accent the outer perimeter of your scrapbook pages and to highlight die-cut letters. Use chalk that has been designed for rubberstamping and scrapbooking to avoid smears.

Designed by Paige Hill

SUPPLIES
Background Cardstock:
    Forest Green
Layout Cardstock: Red
Patterned Paper:
    Ivory Floral
Brads: Gold-toned
Mini Brads: Gold-toned,
    Red
Ribbon Poinsettias & Leaves
Metallic Ribbon: Gold
Adhesive
Journaling: Computer

"Christmas Party"

Brads are primarily used for adhering embellishments to your background cardstock. Use red mini brads as holly berries and gold brads as the center of a poinsettia.

Designed by Karen Delquadro

SUPPLIES
Background Cardstock:
    Blue
Layout Cardstock:
    Pastel Blue, White
Patterned Paper:
    Light Blue with Snowflakes
Rubberstamps: Lower Case Alphabet
Ink Pad: Black
Snowflake Eyelets: White
Punch: Snowflake
Acetate
Embroidery Floss: Metallic Gold
Miniature Santa's Hat
Adhesive
Journaling: Black Marker, Pink Marker

"Reindeer Food"

When you have something on your scrapbook pages that you want to "show off," make a shaker window. The window is made from acetate that has been adhered to the back of a piece of cardstock that has an opening cut in it. Place confetti, oatmeal, or tiny candies in your window—make certain to fill it full enough so you can enjoy the contents, but not so full that the contents cannot move freely inside the window.

Christmas Cards

home for the holidays

recipes

innocence of a child

snow

trimming the tree

memories

angels

Santa

"Christmas 2001"

Designed by Kim Garner

SUPPLIES

Background Cardstock:
Forest Green
Layout Cardstock:
Dark Red, White
Patterned Paper: Red/Green
Christmas Plaid

Eyelets: Green
Metal Letter & Number Charms
Embroidery Floss: Green
Adhesive
Journaling: Computer

What a wonderful Christmas for our entire family. We had a fun morning opening presents from Santa. That night we went to Dad's house for our traditional family party. It was a night full of memories.

2001

Crop several photos into small squares with close-ups of your favorite photo subjects. Make these into Christmas presents simply by adding an embroidery floss bow to the top of each one.

"My 1st Christmas"

Designed by Paige Hill

SUPPLIES
Background Cardstock:
    Floral Wallpaper Pattern
Layout Cardstock: Light Olive
Patterned Paper:
    Red/Tan Gingham
Vellum: Clear
Mini Brads: Gold-toned
Heart Brads: Red
Craft Wire: Gold-toned
Adhesive
Journaling: Computer

Some of the most fun scrapbook pages you can create are ones using photographs of yourself when you were a baby or toddler.

"Patchwork Christmas"

Designed by Kim Garner

SUPPLIES
Background Cardstock:
    Red
Layout Cardstock:
    Forest Green
Patterned Paper:
    Green Checks,
    Green Dots
    Red Checks,
    Red Dots
Alphabet Template
Preprinted Artwork:
    Christmas Assortment
Assorted Buttons:
    Brown, Red
Micro Hole Punch
Embroidery Floss: Green
Adhesive
Journaling: Computer

Use paper pieces or cardstock scraps together to replicate quilting. Use squares or rectangles of similar patterned papers, positioned corner to corner. Add preprinted artwork on top.

"Justine's 2nd Christmas"

Designed by Paige Hill

SUPPLIES
Background Paper:
  Tan with
  Christmas Motifs
Layout Cardstock:
  Green, Red
Patterned Paper:
  Ivory Floral
Preprinted Artwork:
  Christmas Hearts
Paper Punch
Sheer Ribbon: Red
Adhesive
Journaling: Computer

When journaling, keep in mind that your words are going to be read and cherished for years to come. Put extra thought into what you want to express.

"Christmas 1951"

Designed by Karen Delquadro

SUPPLIES
Background Paper:
  Dark Red with
  Fruit Topiaries
Layout Cardstock:
  Metallic Gold Embossed
Patterned Paper:
  Green with Spatters
Handmade Paper: Ivory
Die-cut Letters
Preprinted Artwork:
  Christmas Assortment
Preprinted Frame
Mini Brads: Gold-toned
Adhesive
Journaling: Computer

Place a small scrap of handmade paper behind die-cut letters to accent each one. Handmade paper helps soften the page and works especially well when using vintage photographs.

"Christmas Morn Powder"

Designed by Karen Delquadro

SUPPLIES

Background Cardstock: Kraft
Layout Cardstock: Blue, Brown,
    Green, Olive Green, White
Stickers: Letters & Numbers
Punches: Coffee Mug, Mitten,
    Snowflake
Snowflake Button: White

Fibers: White
Jute: White
Miniature Clothespins
Miniature Coat, Hat, Skis
Adhesive
Journaling: Computer

There are literally hundreds of miniatures on the market today to help you embellish your scrapbook pages. If your budget won't allow for these accessories, almost anything can be created from scraps of cardstock and/or paper.

Designed by Kim Garner

SUPPLIES
Background Cardstock:
    Dark Red
Layout Cardstock:
    Dark Red, Metallic Silver, Tan
Recipe Cards
Gingerbread Eyelets: Brown
Miniature Apron, Chef's Hat,
    Eggs in Carton, Fork,
    Milk Carton, Oven Mitt,
    Spatula, Spoon
Embroidery Floss: White
Adhesive
Journaling: Black Marker

"Baby's 1st Christmas"

Baby's First Christmas

Take a cup of joy and love,
A teaspoonful of laughter,
A heaping dose of lullabyes,
And happy-ever-afters.

Stir in world's of wonder,
And amazing sights & sounds,
Add a sugarplum or two,
'Til happiness abounds.

Sprinkle in some magic,
Ang then sleep 'til morning's light,
And baby's first Christmas,
Will be full of great delight.

—Author Unknown

Designed by Karen Delquadro

SUPPLIES
Background Cardstock:
    Periwinkle
Layout Cardstock:
    Black, Chartreuse, Periwinkle
Rubberstamps: Lower Case Alphabet
Ink Pad: Black
Sticker: Merry Christmas
Star Brad: Gold-toned
Embroidery Floss: Metallic Silver
Glass Beads: Clear
Pewter Word Blocks
Mini Brads: Green
Rhinestone: Green
Adhesive
Journaling: Black Marker

"Family Traditions"

Sometimes you have only a few photographs of a special occasion, but you still want to use them on a double-page scrapbook layout. Be creative so your scrapbook pages won't look too plain keeping in mind that a single photograph can tell the perfect story.

Designed by Paige Hill

SUPPLIES
Background Cardstock: Forest Green
Layout Cardstock: Olive Green
Patterned Papers: Burgundy Argyle,
   Burgundy Suede Renaissance Print
Vellum: Clear
Mini Brads: Red, Silver-toned
Micro Hole Punch
Craft Wire: Silver-toned
Pewter Word Block
Christmas Ornament Charm: Silver-toned
Christmas Tree Charm: Silver-toned
Sheer Ribbon: Olive Green
Adhesive
Journaling: Computer

"Christmas Tree Jubilee"

Scrapbook papers are available with many different textures. When you want a paper with a great amount of "depth" and the appearance of something "rich," use papers that feel like suede.

Designed by Karen Delquadro

SUPPLIES
Background Cardstock: Olive Green
Layout Cardstock: Dark Plum
Stickers: Letters
Pewter Word Blocks
Pewter Snowman Charm
Pewter Wreath Charm
Metal Name Block
Rusted Star Embellishment
Fabric Leaves: Silver
Embroidery Floss: Metallic Silver
Adhesive
Journaling: Computer

"Joy To You"

Try using images of nature on your scrapbook pages. In some instances you can use the "real thing." In other cases it may be necessary to use items that have been man-made, such as leaves made from fabric.

Designed by Kim Garner

SUPPLIES
Background Cardstock:
    Dark Red
Layout Cardstock: Olive Green,
    Dark Red, White
Patterned Paper:
    Red/Green/White Stripes
Precut Tags: Kraft
Punch: 1" Circle
Eyelets: Red
Embroidery Floss: Green, Red
Pewter Word Blocks
Adhesive
Journaling: Computer

"Letters From the North Pole"

Making pockets on your scrapbook pages to hold keepsakes is easy, but effective. Make a large pocket to hold your "letters from Santa" and a smaller pocket to hold additional memorabilia.

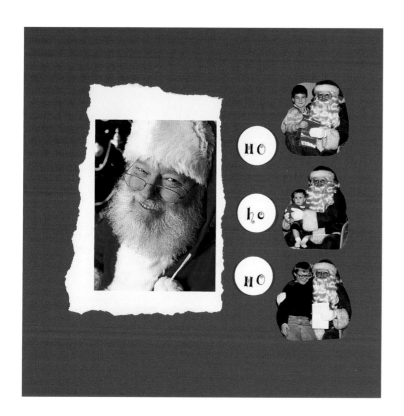

Designed by Karen Delquadro

SUPPLIES
Background Cardstock: Dark Red
Layout Cardstock: Red, Dark Red,
　　White, Recycled White
Stickers: Letters, Christmas Stockings
Mini Brads: Red
Embroidery Floss: Red
Adhesive
Journaling: Computer

"Ho Ho Ho"

When the background in your photographs is extremely busy and tends to take away from the focal point of the photo, simply crop it out. If desired, cut around the main images in the photograph to silhouette your subjects.

... not
A
creature
was
stirring ...
?
?
?

"Merry Christmas 2002"

Designed by Paige Hill

SUPPLIES

Background Cardstock:
  Forest Green
Layout Cardstock:
  Recycled Camel, Red
Handmade Paper: Red
Vellum: Clear, Green
Mini Brads: Silver-toned

Ribbon Poinsettias & Vines
Assorted Beads: Red
Embroidery Floss: Red
Pewter Word Block
Adhesive
Journaling: Computer,
  Black Marker

Incorporate beads into your scrapbook page designs. Use large beads as holly berries and small seed beads around the centers of poinsettia flowers. It is best to hand-sew these beads in place as even the best scrapbook adhesives will not secure them adequately.

"Happy St. Patrick's Day"

Designed by Paige Hill

SUPPLIES

Background Cardstock: Kraft
Layout Cardstock: Dark Olive Green,
   Light Olive Green, White
Patterned Papers: Olive Green with Leaves,
   Sage Green with Swirls
Handmade Paper: Green

Alphabet Template
Mini Brads: Gold-toned
Micro Hole Punch
Raffia: Natural
Adhesive
Journaling: Computer

Use handmade paper to accent specific areas on your scrapbook pages. Tear a small strip and place it across one corner of a photograph or use it to mat your cardstock header.

Cinco de Mayo

We planned our trip to Mazatlan during Cinco de Mayo. It was a huge party! We went to a restaurant that had a really neat show. The dancers were amazing! They were so talented and had such beautiful costumes. After dinner, we all bought sombreros and went to a club. It was so much fun. The only problem we encountered was trying to get our sombreros home on the airplane!

-1989

"Cinco de Mayo"

Designed by Paige Hill

SUPPLIES

Background Cardstock: White
Layout Cardstock: Metallic Gold,
    Green, Ivory, Red
Brads: Black, Green
Paper Punch
Punches: Extra Large Swirl, Large Swirl
Adhesive
Journaling: Computer

Punch several swirls in various sizes from different colors of cardstock. Adhere them in a random pattern on your scrapbook pages.

Kwanzaa

Habari Gani-What's the news? So starts the seven-day holiday called Kwanzaa! This year in Mrs. Andersons fifth grade, the kids learned all about Kwanzaa. They learned of the seven principles of Kwanzaa-one for each day. They are 1. Umoja, or Unity in the family. 2. Kujichagulia, self-determination. 3. Ujima, collective work and responsibility. 4. Ujamaa, Cooperative economics. 5.Nia, Purpose. 6.Kuumba, Creativity. And the last day, 7 is Imani, or faith. The children made tradition Kwanzaa crafts, sang songs and learned of the rich heritage of the people. It was a wonderful lesson!

-2001

"Kwanzaa"

Designed by Paige Hill

SUPPLIES
Background Cardstock: Black
Layout Cardstock: Ivory, Metallic Gold, Green, Red
Brads: Green
Ric-rac: Red
Adhesive
Journaling: Computer

When journaling by computer, the font you choose can be a very important design element. There are many fonts available that have been designed with specific themes in mind and choosing one that is perfect for your scrapbook pages can be as rewarding as finding appropriate decorative elements.

Karen Delquadro

Karen Delquadro is a single mother of one darling daughter, Olivia. Raised in a home where everyone always came home to Grandma's for Christmas, she learned at an early age to appreciate family and cherish family memories.

After the birth of her daughter, she began scrapbooking and this pastime quickly became a passion. Today, Karen says "it" has taken over her small house in Salt Lake City, Utah, but she considers the relationship a healthy one—her scrapbooks, her supplies, and herself.

Delquadro loves being able to share her love for scrapbooking with Olivia, who is five years old. They sit together and look at the baby pictures in her scrapbooks, or while Delquadro is designing new scrapbook pages, her daughter creates in her very own way. She says she often gets lost in her creativity and feels less guilty than she would if it were chocolate—but that's another story!

Delquadro is the author of *Scrapbooking Childhood Moments*, published by Sterling/Chapelle.

Kim Garner

Kim Garner loves to scrapbook family memories and has been creating personal scrapbook designs for seven years. Garner is especially interested in simple, but classic designs using embellishments such as: eyelets, fibers, tags, and charms.

A teacher by profession, she loves sharing her creative ideas with friends and family. Garner also enjoys children's and adult literature, home organization and decoration, Broadway musicals, and movie theater popcorn!

She loves living in Roy, Utah with her husband, Craig, and her two children, Christian and Sydnee.

Paige Hill

Paige Hill has always been a "crafty" person. When she was a child, she loved to help her mom decorate the house for the holidays. At Halloween, she would set up little displays in the windows with her toys.

As Hill grew, her interest in art did also. She studied Fashion Merchandising in college where she met her husband, Bruce. They married and soon after she decided to start a crafting business with her parents, selling tole-painted furniture and home accessories.

In 2000, Hill's mother gave her a photo album containing old, faded photographs of her grandparents. Practically ruined, she decided to restore the album. This endeavor lead to the creation of several albums of her three children so they can always remember the joys in their childhood.

In addition to scrapbooking and tole painting, Hill enjoys sewing, quilting, and interior design. With her family, she enjoys traveling, camping, hiking, and just being outdoors. She resides in North Ogden, Utah.

INCHES TO MILLIMETRES AND CENTIMETRES
MM-Millimetres   CM-Centimetres

INCHES	MM	CM	INCHES	CM	INCHES	CM
$1/8$	3	0.9	9	22.9	30	76.2
$1/4$	6	0.6	10	25.4	31	78.7
$3/8$	10	1.0	11	27.9	32	81.3
$1/2$	13	1.3	12	30.5	33	83.8
$5/8$	16	1.6	13	33.0	34	86.4
$3/4$	19	1.9	14	35.6	35	88.9
$7/8$	22	2.2	15	38.1	36	91.4
1	25	2.5	16	40.6	37	94.0
$1 1/4$	32	3.2	17	43.2	38	96.5
$1 1/2$	38	3.8	18	45.7	39	99.1
$1 3/4$	44	4.4	19	48.3	40	101.6
2	51	5.1	20	50.8	41	104.1
$2 1/2$	64	6.4	21	53.3	42	106.7
3	76	7.6	22	55.9	43	109.2
$3 1/2$	89	8.9	23	58.4	44	111.8
4	102	10.2	24	61.0	45	114.3
$4 1/2$	114	11.4	25	63.5	46	116.8
5	127	12.7	26	66.0	47	119.4
6	152	15.2	27	68.6	48	121.9
7	178	17.8	28	71.1	49	124.5
8	203	20.3	29	73.7	50	127.0

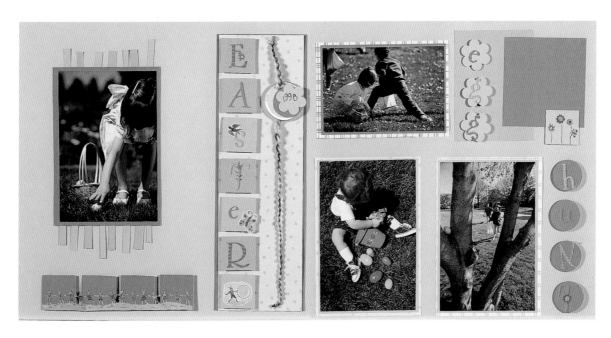

INDEX

8/07